AF605675
N
W
E
S
QLD
QUEENSLAND
SA
SOUTH
AUSTRALIA
NSW
NEW SOUTH WALES
VIC
VICTORIA
ACT
AUSTRALIAN
CAPITAL
TERRITORY
TAS
TASMANIA

KYLE SURRY
KIDS' GUIDE TO AUSTRALIA'S STATES & TERRITORIES
DISCOVERING
SA
SOUTH AUSTRALIA
REDBACK
publishing

First Published 2026 by
Redback Publishing
Suite 6, 13a Narabang Way,
Belrose NSW 2085
Australia

www.redbackpublishing.com
orders@redbackpublishing.com

ISBN 978-1-761400-64-3

Author: Kyle Surry
Editors: Lucinda Dodds and Emma Dobinson
Designer: Redback Publishing

MIX
Paper from responsible sources
FSC™ C001507
FSC www.fsc.org

Original illustrations © Redback Publishing 2026
Originated by Redback Publishing

Acknowledgements
Abbreviations: l—left, r—right, b—bottom, t—top, c—centre, m—middle
We would like to thank the following for permission to reproduce photographs: (Images © shutterstock, Alamy) p6-7 - Charles Hill (1824 - 1915) (Australia) Born in Coventry, Great Britain. Died in Adelaide. Details on Google Art Project - NAHnyRi288qtAg at Google Cultural Institute maximum zoom level, Public Domain, https://commons.wikimedia.org/w/index.php?curid=23601305, p7rm - Cynthia A Jackson / Shutterstock.com, p23ml - mastersky / Shutterstock.com, p29ml - Squiresy92 - Own work, CC BY-SA 4.0, https://commons.wikimedia.org/w/index.php?curid=48419387, p30 - Alexandre.ROSA / Shutterstock.com

NATIONAL LIBRARY OF AUSTRALIA
A catalogue record for this book is available from the National Library of Australia

CONTENTS

Kati Thanda-Lake Eyre

A LONG TIME AGO

Who Was There First?

The Kaurna people were living in the Adelaide area long before settlers from Europe arrived.

Across the rest of South Australia, there is evidence that Indigenous Australians were living there thousands of years ago. Rock engravings in the Olary region of South Australia may be over 35,000 years old.

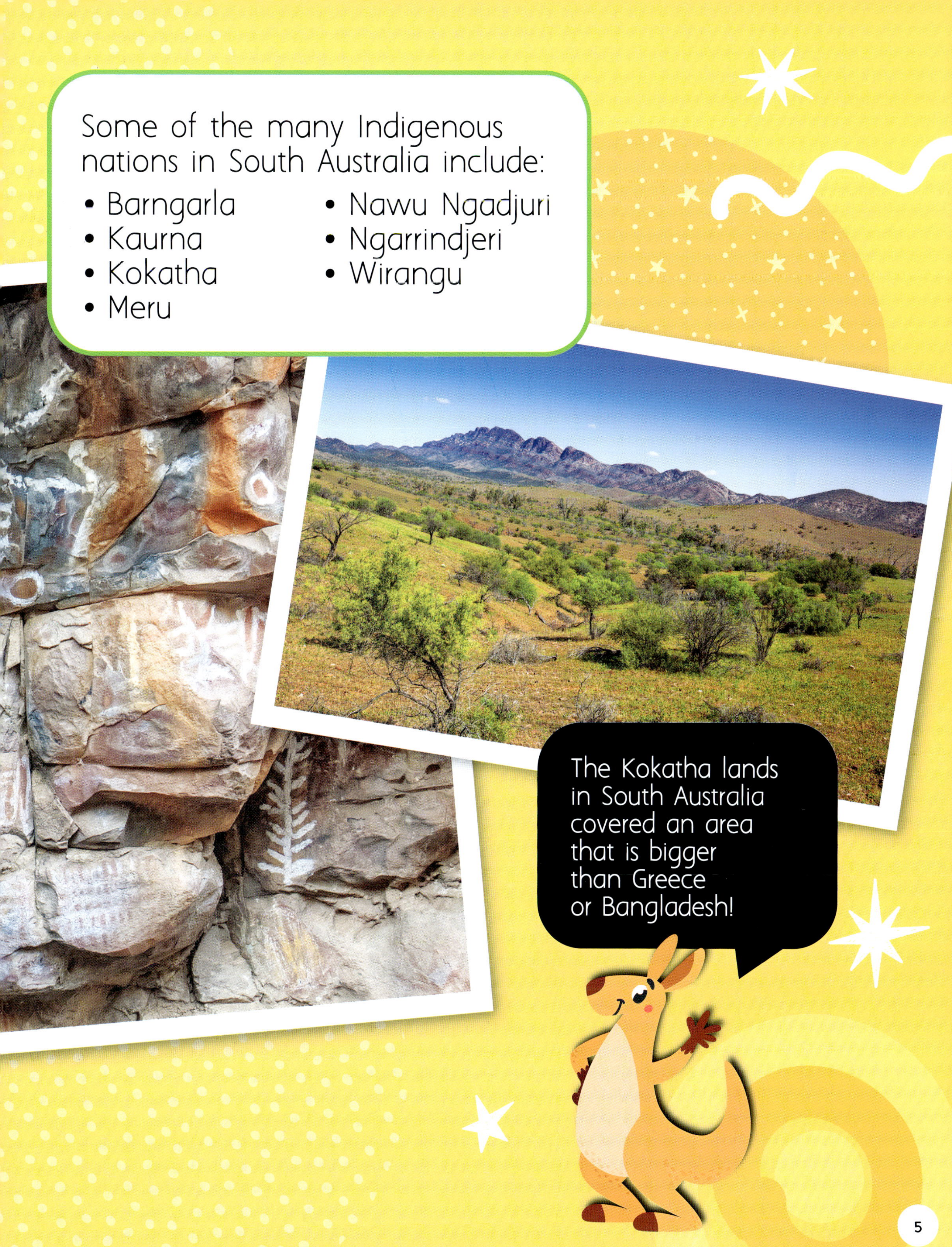

Some of the many Indigenous nations in South Australia include:

- Barngarla
- Kaurna
- Kokatha
- Meru
- Nawu Ngadjuri
- Ngarrindjeri
- Wirangu

The Kokatha lands in South Australia covered an area that is bigger than Greece or Bangladesh!

SETTLERS FROM BRITAIN

No convicts were sent to South Australia, making it unique amongst all the early Australian colonies. The first British colonists who sailed to South Australia were all free immigrants.

Proclamation Day

In 1836, the settlers from Britain arrived at Kangaroo Island after an eight month journey on nine ships.

Governor Hindmarsh held a ceremony to mark the founding of South Australia. The holiday now called Proclamation Day is a reminder of that event.

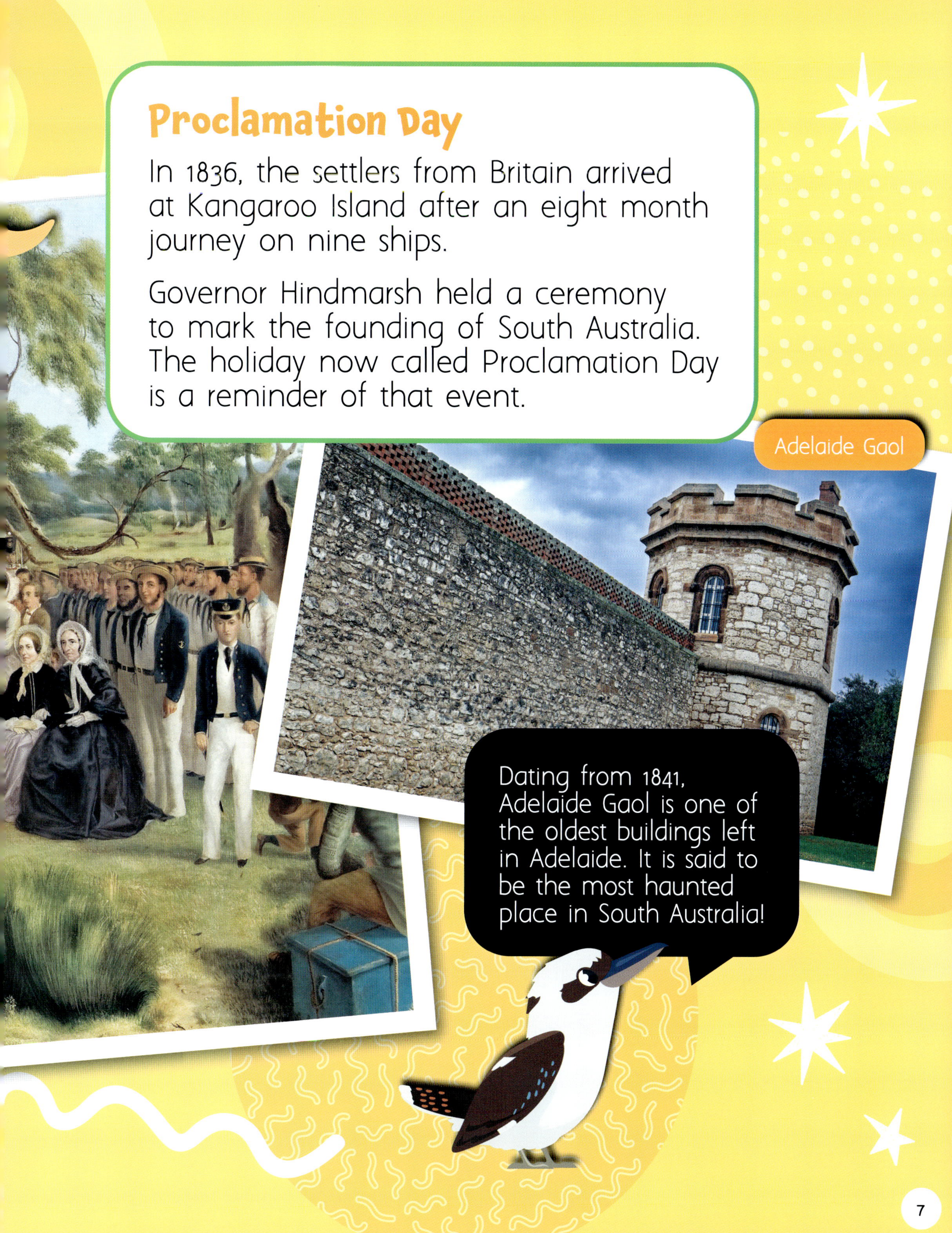

Adelaide Gaol

WHERE IS SOUTH AUSTRALIA?

South Australia is the third largest of Australia's states by area.

The capital city is Adelaide, located on the River Torrens. South Australia's shortened name is written as SA.

Where are the borders of South Australia?

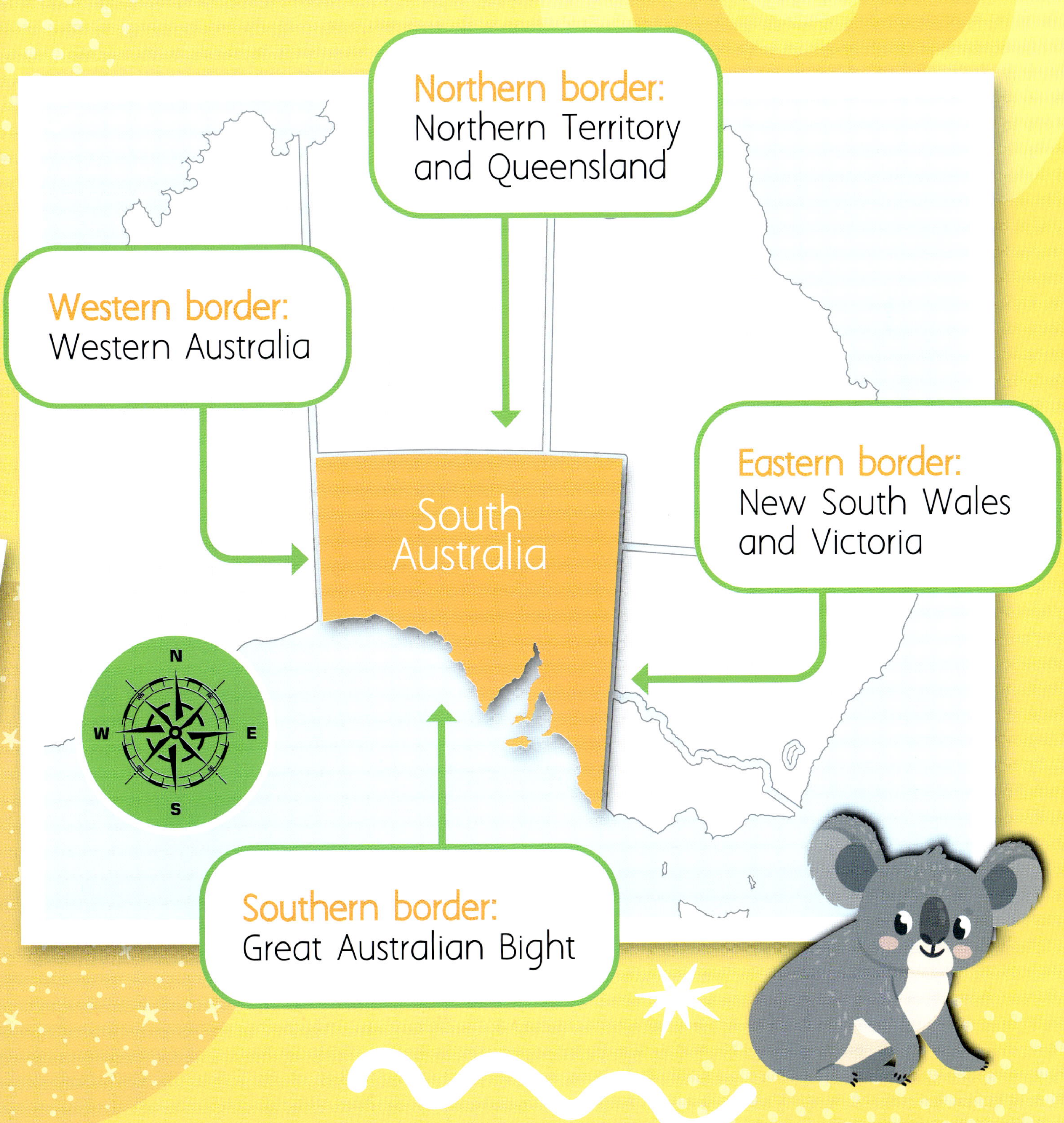

PLACES IN SOUTH AUSTRALIA

Fleurieu Peninsula

The Adelaide Hills, in the Mount Lofty Ranges, form part of the Fleurieu Peninsula.

Barossa Valley

Northeast of Adelaide, the Barossa Valley has been a wine producing region since the 1800s.

Kangaroo Island

Kangaroo Island is Australia's third largest island.

Far North

The Far North reaches to the border with the Northern Territory. This region is very arid.

Eyre Peninsula

The Eyre Peninsula's economy depends on agriculture and tourism.

Nullarbor Plain

This is a vast, arid region along the southern coast.

KATI THANDA-LAKE EYRE

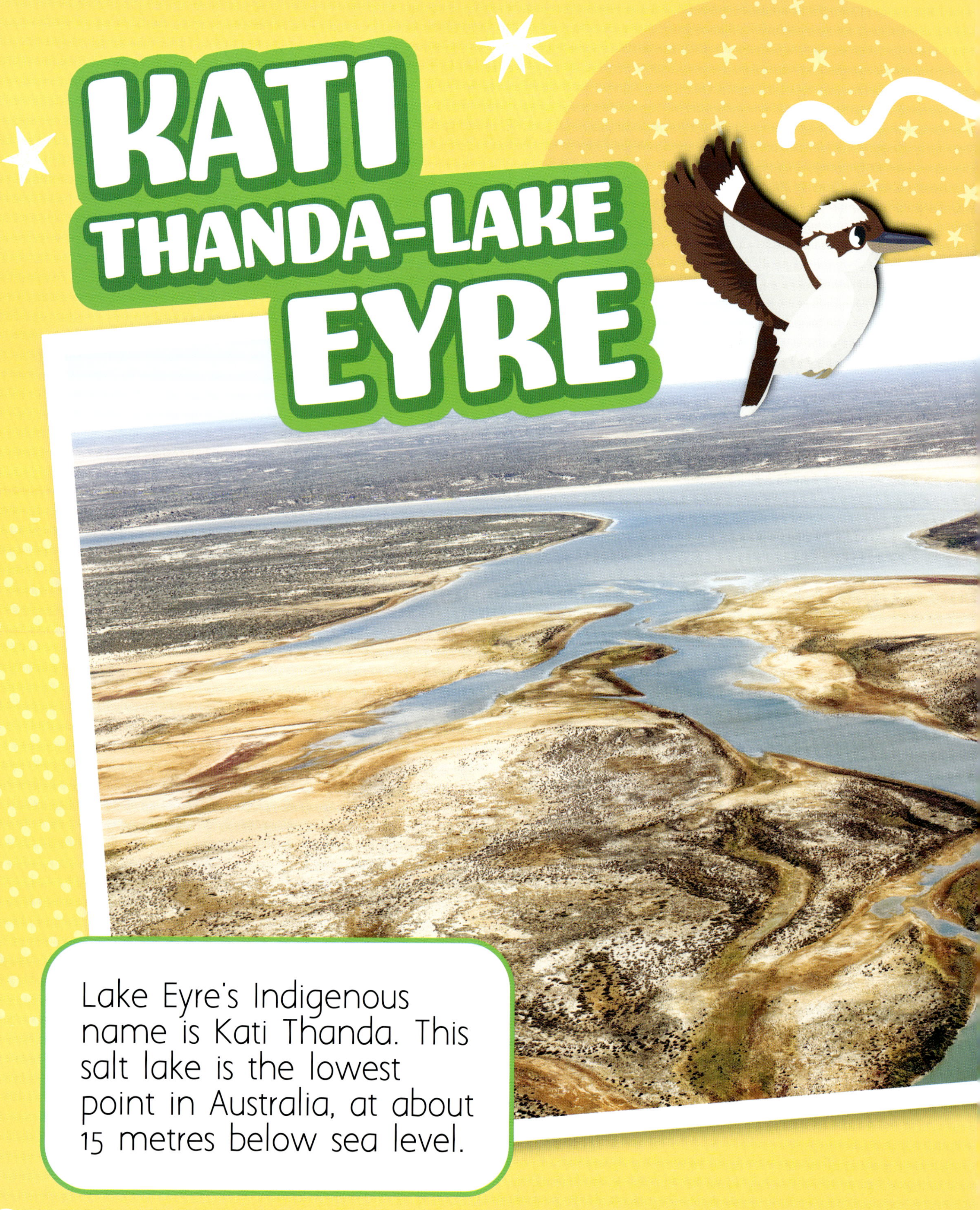

Lake Eyre's Indigenous name is Kati Thanda. This salt lake is the lowest point in Australia, at about 15 metres below sea level.

Most of the time this salt lake is dry, but it sometimes fills with water. Thousands of waterbirds then migrate to it. No-one is sure how the birds know that the lake is full of water, but some of them have flown long distances to get there.

PEOPLE IN SOUTH AUSTRALIA

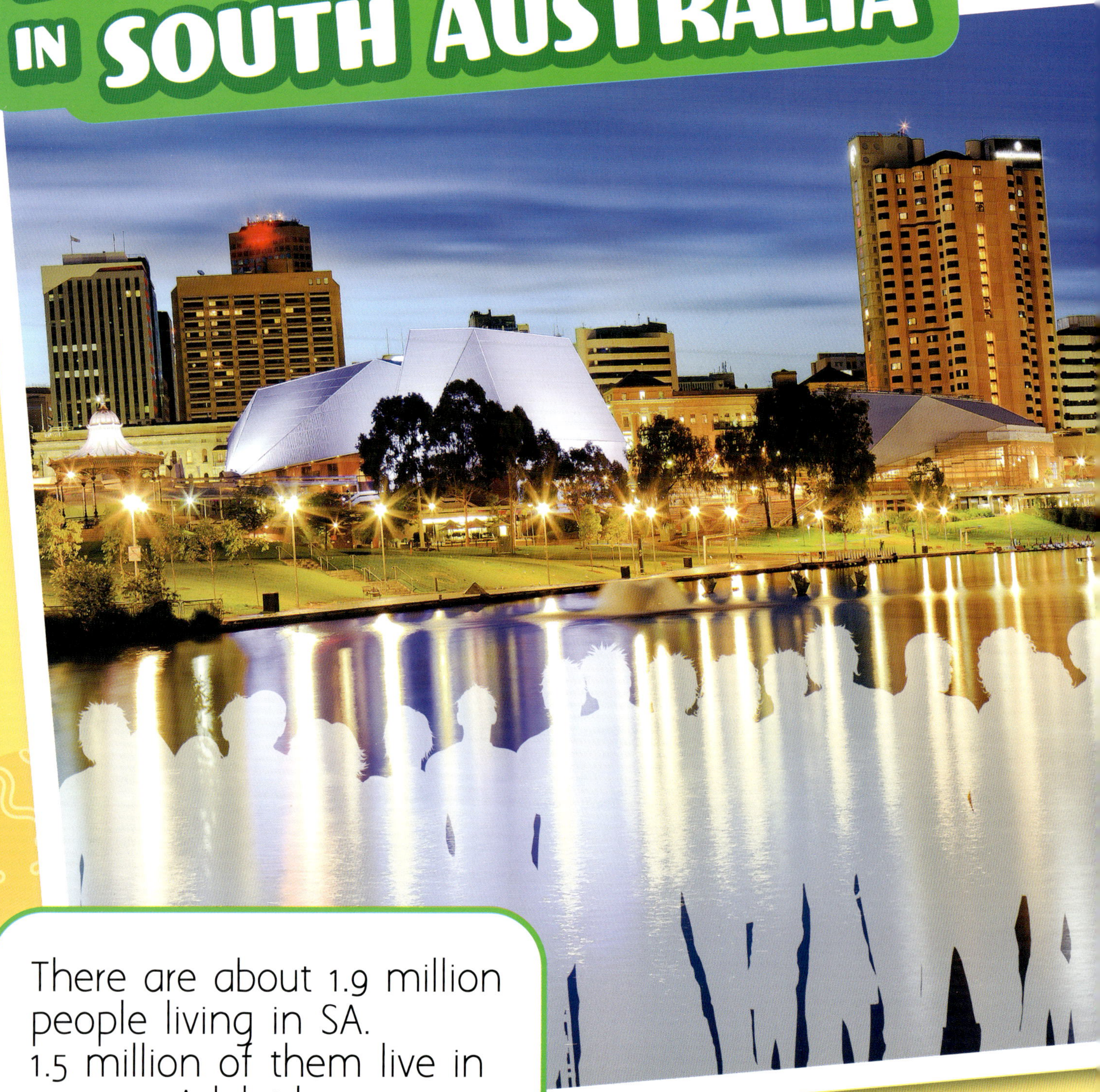

There are about 1.9 million people living in SA.
1.5 million of them live in or near Adelaide.

After Adelaide, the next largest towns are Mount Gambier, Gawler and Mount Barker.

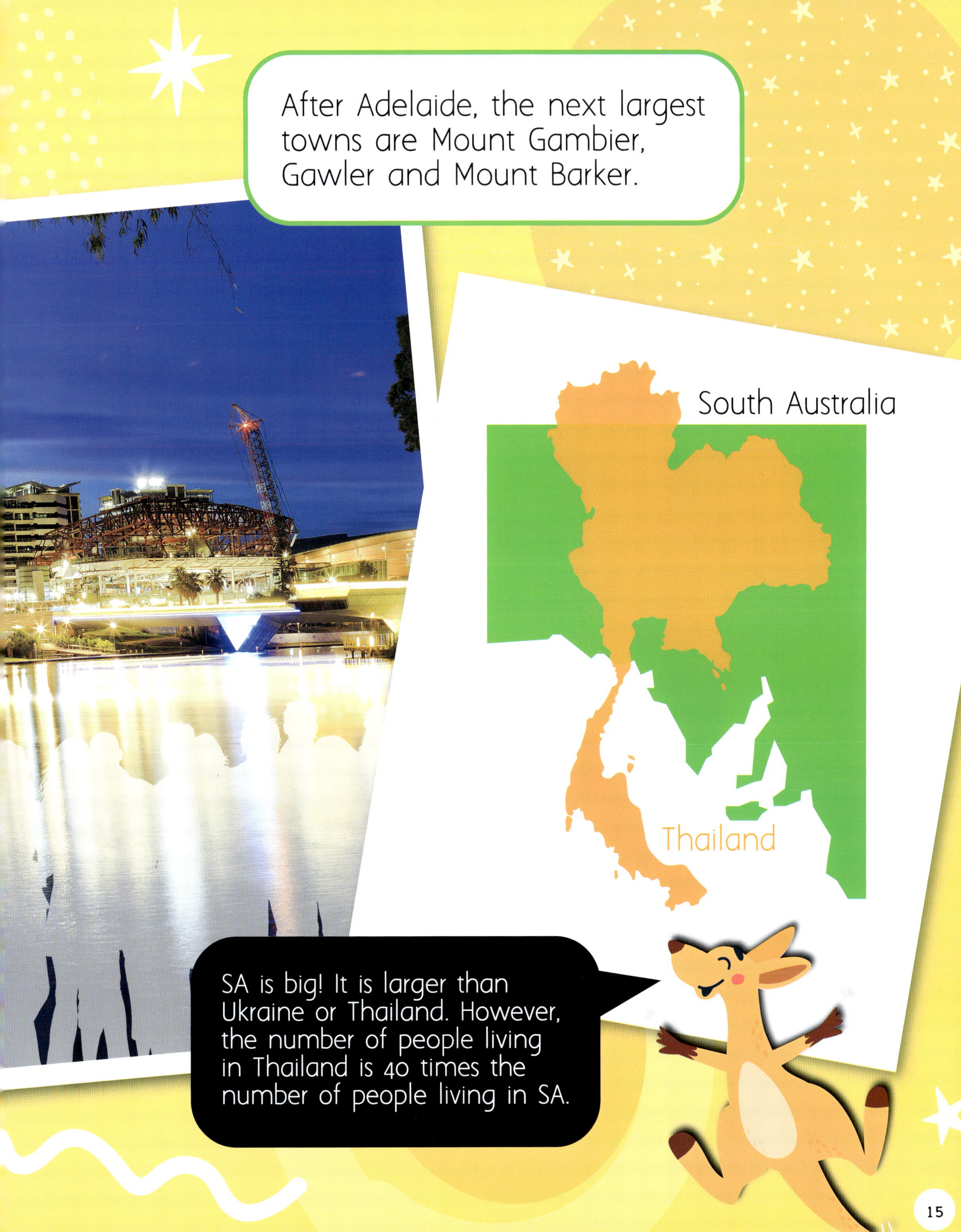

SA is big! It is larger than Ukraine or Thailand. However, the number of people living in Thailand is 40 times the number of people living in SA.

PEOPLE NEED WATER

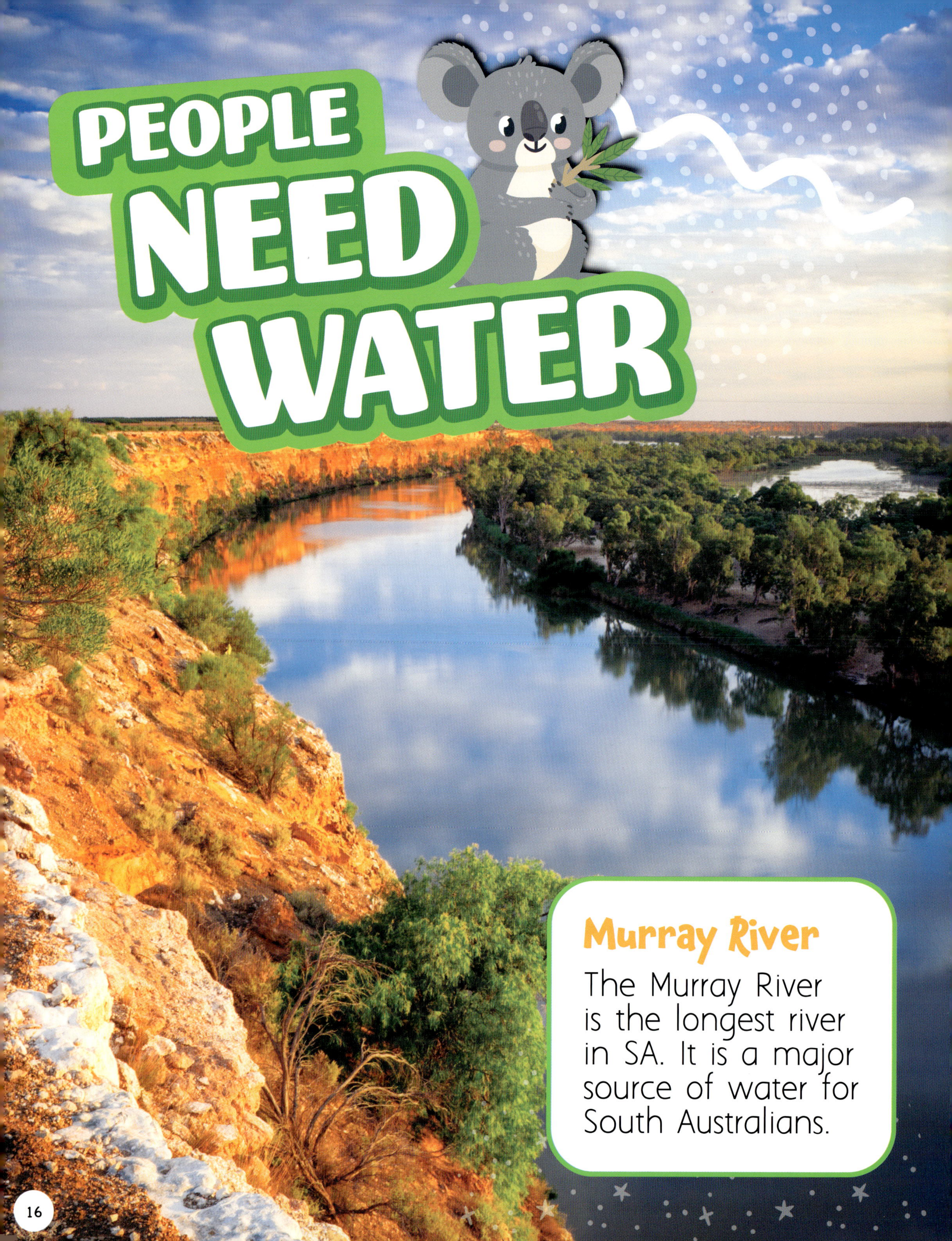

Murray River

The Murray River is the longest river in SA. It is a major source of water for South Australians.

River Torrens

The River Torrens provided the first colonial settlers with a source of fresh water.

Artesian Basins

Artesian basins are sources of water deep under the ground. Some of these basins are the size of huge seas. There are large artesian basins under South Australia. Their water comes to the surface in desert areas as springs, but people also dig wells to reach the artesian water.

Transport

Using canoes, rowboats, sailing ships and paddle steamboats, both the Indigenous Australians and the settlers used rivers for transport.

GREAT AUSTRALIAN BIGHT

The coast of South Australia follows part of the Great Australian Bight and faces the Southern Ocean.

The ocean floor is not very deep in the Great Australia Bight. Just a few thousand years ago, it was dry land. This was before sea levels rose around the world after the end of the last Ice Age.

The Nullarbor Plain is an arid region of limestone plains that cover an area twice as big as Tasmania. Under the surface are hundreds of caves, some of them full of water.

The cliffs along the coast of the Great Australian Bight are made of the same limestone that forms the rest of the Nullarbor Plain.

The word *Nullarbor* is Latin. It means having no trees.

DESERTS IN SOUTH AUSTRALIA

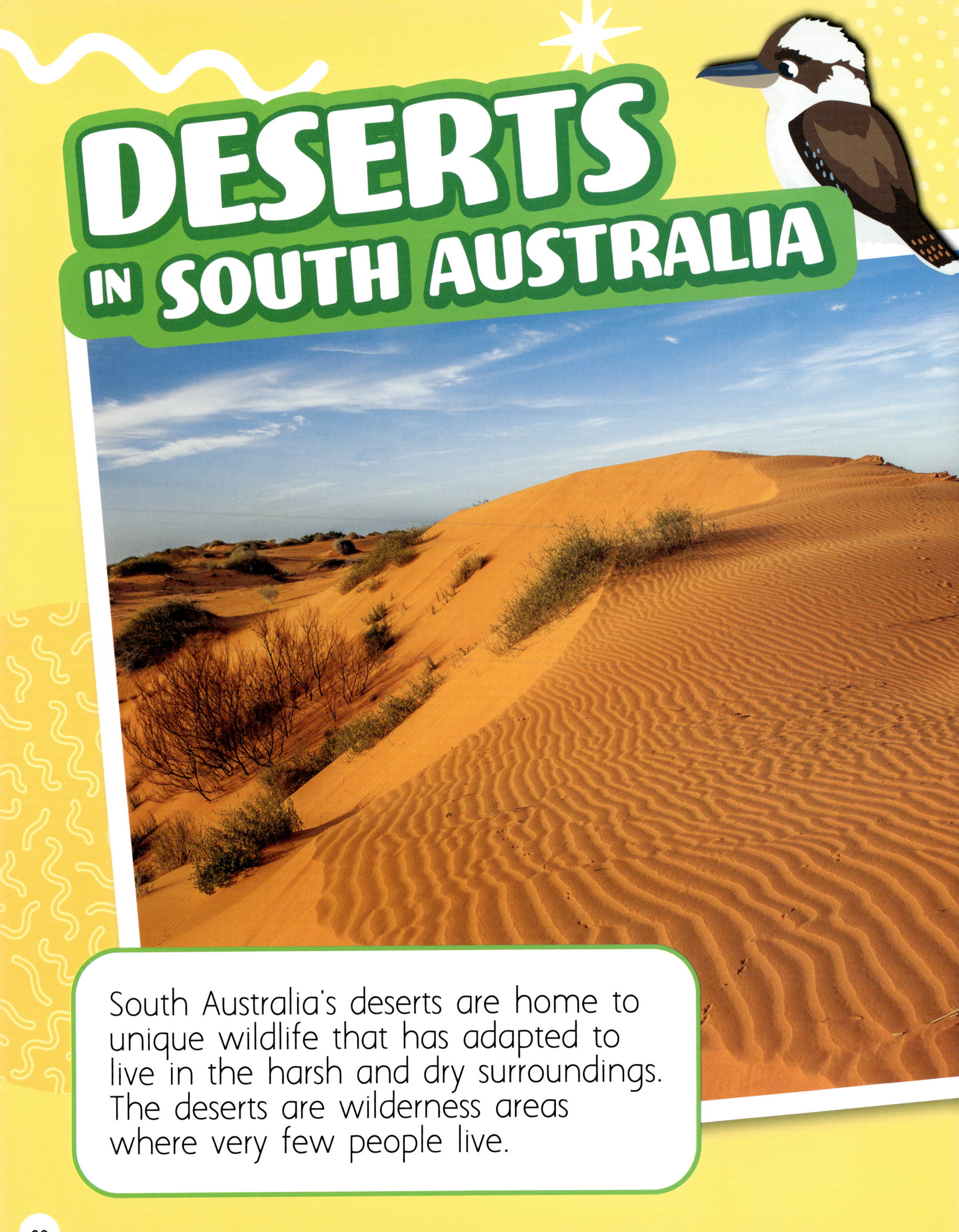

South Australia's deserts are home to unique wildlife that has adapted to live in the harsh and dry surroundings. The deserts are wilderness areas where very few people live.

Some of the many deserts in South Australia include:

- Great Victoria Desert
- Strzelecki Desert
- Sturt Stony Desert
- Tirari Desert
- Pedirka Desert
- Simpson Desert

Great Victoria Desert

Surprisingly, there is underground water deep beneath many of the deserts.

Sturt Stony Desert

TRAINS AND TELEGRAPH LINES SOUTH TO NORTH

Overland Telegraph Line

In 1872, the completion of the Overland Telegraph, linking Darwin and Adelaide, made SA the first Australian colony to be linked to London by telegraph.

Suddenly people no longer had to wait months for a letter to reach Britain by ship. They could now use the telegraph and send a message immediately.

The Ghan

The Ghan is the train that runs between Adelaide and Darwin. The deserts formed a natural barrier that separated the colonial settlements around the coast. When the railway line from Adelaide to Darwin was finally finished, this journey became much faster and safer.

Building of the railway line began in 1877 at Port Augusta, but it did not finally reach Darwin until 2004.

The Ghan is named after the Afghan cameleers who helped to build the railway line.

MINING IN SOUTH AUSTRALIA

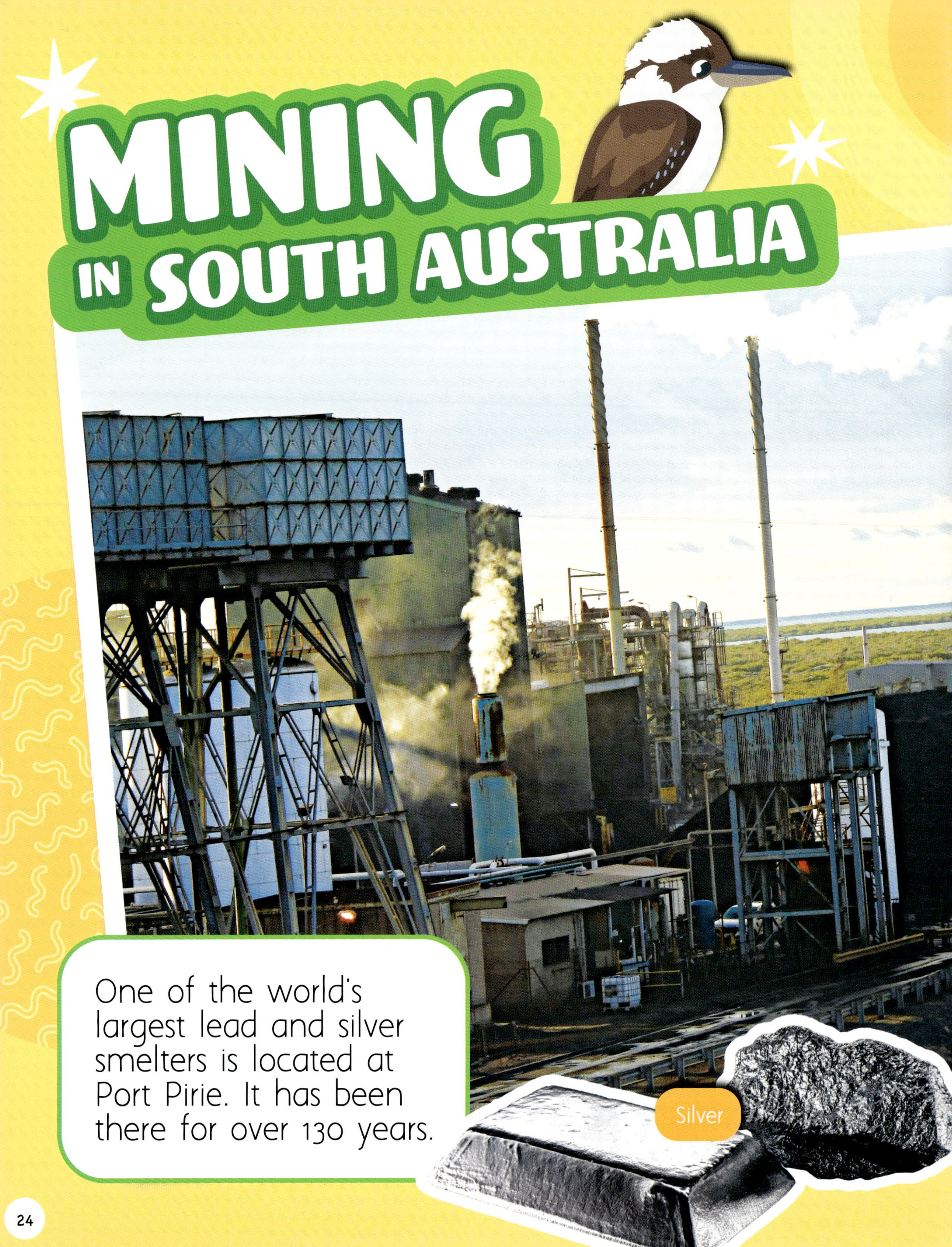

One of the world's largest lead and silver smelters is located at Port Pirie. It has been there for over 130 years.

The Olympic Dam deposits of copper, uranium, gold and silver are one of the largest collections of ores known to exist anywhere in the world.

Uranium ore from SA helps to make Australia one of the world's largest exporters of uranium. Other countries use this uranium to generate their electricity.

Opal is mined at Andamooka and Coober Pedy.

GOVERNMENT OF SOUTH AUSTRALIA

South Australia's first Council Chamber was opened in 1843.

In 1857, SA gained its own colonial Parliament. Six years later, in 1863, the Northern Territory became the electorate of Flinders when it was added to SA.

In 1901, Federation created the state of South Australia.

The South Australian Parliament Today

The House of Assembly (Upper House) has 47 members.

The Legislative Council (Lower House) has 22 members.

SA parliament house in Adelaide

Legislative Council Chamber, 1950

In 1894, SA became the first place in Australia, and one of the first in the world, to allow women to vote and to stand for election to Parliament.

SOUTH AUSTRALIAN FLAGS

Australian Aboriginal Flag

The Aboriginal Flag was first flown in 1971. It was designed by elder Harold Thomas in 1970.

What the flag represents:

Yellow Disc	The Sun and yellow ochre
Red	The land
Black	The Aboriginal people of Australia

SA State Flag

The state flag dates from 1904. The Union Jack on the flag is a reminder of South Australia's historic ties with Britain. The badge shows the piping shrike, a South Australian bird. It sits on a gumtree branch and behind it is a golden circle, representing the rising Sun.

EMBLEMS OF SOUTH AUSTRALIA

Floral Emblem
Sturt's desert pea

Animal Emblem
Hairy-nosed wombat

Gemstone Emblem
Opal

Fossil Emblem
Spriggina Floundersi

Mineral Emblem
Bornite

Marine Emblem
Leafy sea dragon

The Coat of Arms

The Coat of Arms is a symbol of SA and each part of it has a meaning:

Piping shrike
A South Australian bird

Sturt's desert pea
The state flower

Wheat, barley and fruits
Represent agriculture

Cog wheels
Represent industry

Miner's pick
Represents mining

FOSSILS AT NARACOORTE

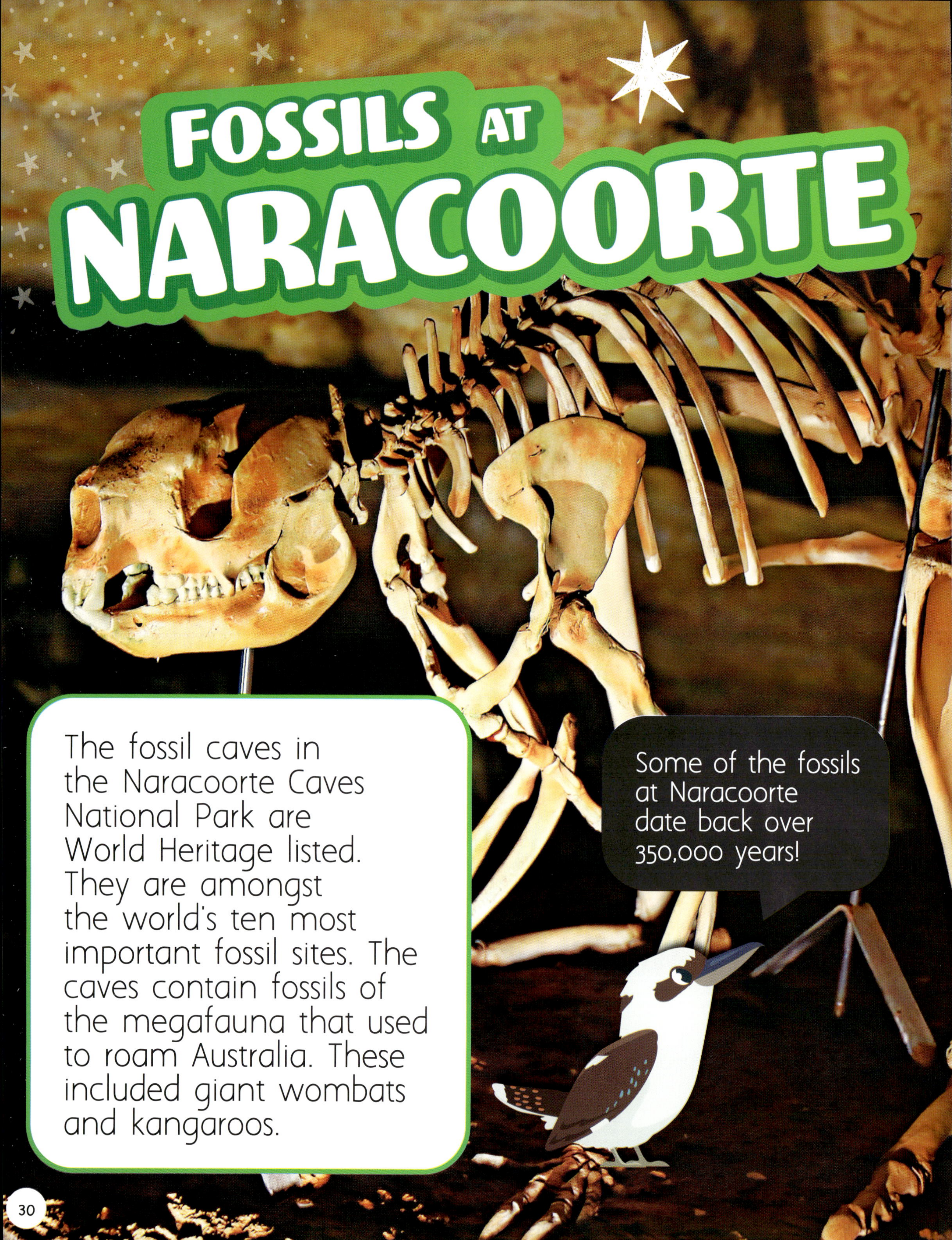

The fossil caves in the Naracoorte Caves National Park are World Heritage listed. They are amongst the world's ten most important fossil sites. The caves contain fossils of the megafauna that used to roam Australia. These included giant wombats and kangaroos.

GLOSSARY

arid having low rainfall

colonists people who move to a new country and impose their culture on it

Ice Age time in the past when much of the Earth was covered in ice and snow

Latin ancient language often used in science

limestone white rock that formed under the sea

motto few words that describe a group or country's ideals

settlers people who move to live in a different country, usually as farmers

smelter factory for getting metal out of ores

telegraph system for sending messages using electricity and wires

Mount Gambier

INDEX

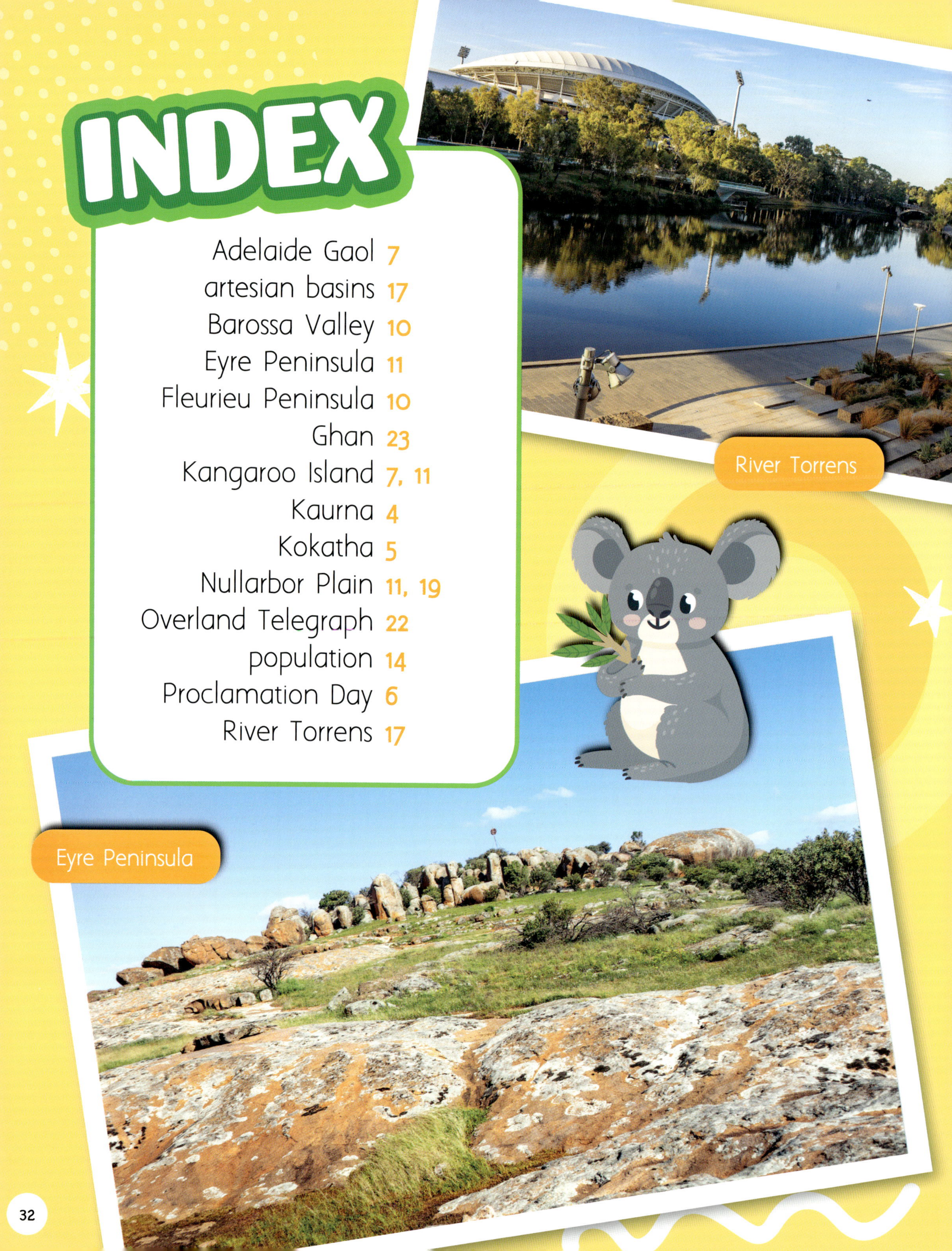

River Torrens

Eyre Peninsula

KIDS' GUIDE
TO
AUSTRALIA'S
STATES & TERRITORIES
NT
NORTHERN
TERRITORY
WA
WESTERN
AUSTRALIA